# The First Modern Olympics

By LaVada Weir

The first Olympic Games were held in Greece almost three thousand years ago. Every four years Greek athletes would gather to compete for fame and honor, especially in running.

When the modern Olympics began in 1896, it was fitting that the games should begin again in Greece.

Sixty thousand spectators filled the new marble stadium of Herodes Atticus in Athens. Greek citizens, determined to get a look at "their" games, covered the surrounding hillsides. In the royal reviewing box appeared King George of Greece, dressed in full military regalia. The queen was dressed all in white, and the royal princess wore bright-colored diplomatic bands.

Inside the stadium athletes from thirteen countries—Australia, Austria, Bulgaria, Chile, Denmark, England, France, Germany, Greece, Hungary, Sweden, Switzerland, and the United States—assembled for the opening ceremony.

As head of the host country, King George of Greece spoke the words that have begun every Olympiad since: "I declare the opening of the Olympic Games."

One athlete stepped forward and took the Olympic oath on behalf of all the competitors: "In the name of all competitors I promise that, in the Olympic Games, we shall respect the rules as honest sportsmen and that we shall participate in the spirit of fairness for the glory of the sport and the honor of our teams."

Twelve track-and-field events, including the

> **Unbeatable Al**
> The only person to win four consecutive gold medals in the same event is discus thrower Al Oerter of the United States. Oerter won the discus at the 1956, 1960, 1964, and 1968 Games. And he set a new record each time!

marathon, were held, plus swimming, gymnastics, wrestling, lawn tennis, weight lifting, shooting, fencing, and cycling.

The team from the United States was small, made up of only a ten-man track team, two riflemen, and one swimmer. The members paid all their own expenses to get there. They received no support from their government. Nevertheless, they were successful, particularly in the track events.

The first person in the modern Olympics to win a first-place medal was Jim Connolly from the United States for the hop, step, and jump, now known as the triple jump. Today we would say that he won a gold medal, but in these first games the medals were actually silver.

The United States team continued to gather first-place medals, with victories in the 100-meter run, the 400-meter run, the 110-meter hurdles, the broad jump, the high jump, the pole vault, and the shot put. They were picking up second-place medals, too.

The Greeks were disappointed to see foreigners winning events that had their origins in Greece. But they felt confident that their athletes would win the next event, the discus throw.

Bob Garrett of the United States entered the discus. He had never thrown a genuine discus before. At home at Princeton University he had seen a picture of one, and a friend who was good at metalwork made one for him. Now, when he picked up the real thing for the first time in the Athens stadium, he realized that it was much lighter than what he was used to. Garrett threw the discus farther than he had ever thrown before and farther than anyone else could throw it in that first modern Olympics.

The Greeks were now more crestfallen. Their only hope lay in winning the marathon. A special trophy had been donated to be presented to the winner. This trophy meant more than just winning the race; it represented Greek history. They pinned their hopes on a twenty-five-year-old shepherd, Spyridon Louis. The shepherd had only chanced to hear of the Olympics. Liking to run and wanting to help his country if he could, he entered.

On April 10, 1896, twenty-five runners lined up at the town of Marathon. At two o'clock a Greek army officer gave the signal, and the runners started on the historic trail to Athens that Pheidippides had run nearly twenty-four centuries before.

Greek peasants lined the way solidly, expecting to see Louis leading. But instead they saw a Frenchman, followed by an American and an Australian. When Louis entered the village of Pikermi, he was told how many were ahead of him. Louis had fasted the day before, and he had spent the night in prayer. "Do not fear," he told spectators. "I will overtake them."

Twenty-three kilometers from Marathon, the American dropped from exhaustion. At thirty-two kilometers, the Frenchman collapsed. The Greek shepherd kept pounding away. He caught up with the Australian, who was tiring. Louis passed him. The roar of the crowd now traveled with him. There were still more than three kilometers to go. A messenger on horseback was sent ahead with the news. The king's two sons rushed from their royal box down to the arena. When the shepherd entered the stadium, the crowd stood cheering. As soon as Louis crossed the finish line, the two princes picked him up and carried him on their shoulders to their father. The crowd went wild.

Everyone wanted to give something to Louis—from women who thrust jewels upon him to a bootblack who promised to shine his shoes free for the rest of his life. On the last day of the Games the grand parade of the victors was led by Spyridon Louis, who carried an olive branch, his trophy, his first-place medal, and a Greek flag.

# Olympic Challenge

1. The first modern Olympic Games were held in Greece in what year?
   a) 1775
   b) 1896
   c) 1930
   d) 1970

2. The Olympic event that includes five different sports is the
   a) marathon
   b) decathlon
   c) modern pentathlon
   d) relay race

3. The Olympic event that features foils is
   a) archery
   b) volleyball
   c) diving
   d) fencing

4. In which Olympic event would you see an athlete do a snatch?
   a) relay racing
   b) weight lifting
   c) ice-skating
   d) high jump

5. Which of these is not an Olympic sport?
   a) lacrosse
   b) water polo
   c) archery
   d) swimming

6. The Olympic event in which you would find competitors luffing and tacking is
   a) skiing
   b) long jump
   c) cycling
   d) yacht racing

7. The Olympic sport in which team members rotate positions is
   a) basketball
   b) equestrian
   c) volleyball
   d) gymnastics

8. In the shot put, competitors win by hurling a metal ball
   a) into a basket
   b) the shortest distance
   c) into the strike zone
   d) the longest distance

9. The decathlon includes ten events in one. Which of these events is not a part of the decathlon?
   a) long jump
   b) high jump
   c) steeplechase
   d) pole vault

10. The Olympic event in which it is a foul to hold the ball underwater when tackled is
    a) water polo
    b) swimming
    c) diving
    d) rowing

Illustrated by Ed King

Answers on page 48.

# The Jim Thorpe Story

**His remarkable athletic performances grew from a boyhood love for sports**

By Nancy Smiler Levinson

Our country has had many great athletes, but there is one who is considered the greatest all-around athlete of them all. His name—Jim Thorpe.

Jim was best known for his Olympic championship in track and field. But his winning record did not stop there. He also won wide fame in both football and baseball.

In the 1912 Olympic Games Jim stunned the sports world by winning both the decathlon and pentathlon. But because of a rule infraction Jim had to surrender his trophies.

It was not until almost thirty years after his death that a new Olympic committee voted to return these awards to his family.

James Francis Thorpe was born on May 28, 1888, in the Indian territory that is now part of the state of Oklahoma. His father was half Irish and half Sac and Fox Indian. His mother, who was part French, was the granddaughter of a famous and noble

Chippewa chief, Black Hawk.

Jim's tribal name, *Wa Tho Huck*, means Bright Path.

His love for sports began when he was very young. Before he started school, he knew how to swim, ride horseback, and even hunt. It seemed that every time he tried a new sport he did it well.

Jim grew up in a large family. He had a twin brother, Charles, and as the boys grew up on the Sac and Fox reservation, they spent many hours together racing, wrestling, and camping. They were not only twins but best friends as well.

Sadly, however, Charles became ill and died when he was nine. It was a terrible blow to Jim. For a long time afterward he remained a loner.

When Jim was sixteen, he was sent from the reservation to further his education at the Carlisle Indian School in Carlisle, a small town in Pennsylvania.

While Jim was attending the Carlisle school, his powerful athletic ability was discovered, and he was promptly placed on the football team, the Hotshots.

One day he happened to notice some boys working out in track and field. They were practicing the high jump. This was something new to Jim. Interested, he stopped to watch and decided to try it, too. The high-jump bar was placed at five feet, nine inches, and although he was warned that it was much too high for a newcomer, he tried it anyway—and made it!

Watching from the sideline was the school's coach, Glenn "Pop" Warner. Pop was astonished at what Jim had done and immediately offered to coach him in track-and-field skills.

In game after game on the football field he continued to amaze people, and he won almost every track-and-field event he entered.

Jim had now grown to nearly six feet tall and had become the talk of Pennsylvania.

> **Youthful Champion**
> Bob Mathias of the United States was only seventeen years old when he won the decathlon title at the 1948 Olympics in London, England. Mathias also won the decathlon gold medal at the 1952 Games in Helsinki, Finland. He later served as a U.S. Congressman.

Sometimes, though, his life did not run as smoothly as his races. He did not always like to practice and follow rules.

Jim was learning that being a hero did not necessarily bring happiness.

During the summers of 1909 and 1910, Jim tried yet another sport—baseball. He joined the Carolina League and played for the Rocky Mount Club, earning about twenty dollars a week. He had never pitched before, but the first time he tried, he pitched a 4-0 shutout. In that season he pitched 25 games and won 23!

Pop Warner urged Jim to return to Pennsylvania, promising to train him for a very special event—the Olympics.

He trained hard and for long hours, but he also continued to play football for the Carlisle team. When he brought the football team to victory over the unbeaten Harvard University team, Jim became a national hero. He was chosen an All-American halfback for the first time in 1911, and again in 1912.

Then with the Olympic Games of 1912, held in Stockholm, Sweden, came the highlight of Jim's career. Jim Thorpe won both the decathlon and the pentathlon.

When the awards were presented, King Gustav V of Sweden called Jim "the greatest athlete in the world."

This was truly a bright and happy time for Jim, but unfortunately it did not last long. According to the Olympic rules, competitors in the games must be amateurs, athletes who don't earn money at their sport. News of Jim's earlier baseball days was made public. Because he had earned a few dollars a game, the Olympic committee decided he had been a semiprofessional athlete, and his name and accomplishments were removed from the Olympic records. Two other contestants were declared the winners of the decathlon and pentathlon.

"I did not play for the money that was in it," Jim tried to explain, "but because I like to play ball." It did no good, however. He had to return his awards.

Jim left Carlisle in 1913. He went on to play professional baseball and football, and he helped organize what was to become the National Football League.

In 1950, after many years of being out of the sports spotlight, Jim was recognized once again. A newspaper association polled nearly four hundred sportswriters, and Jim was named the greatest football player as well as the greatest male athlete of the first half of the century.

Three years after that recognition, Jim Thorpe died. But that was not the final chapter in the story of his life. In 1982 a new Olympic committee voted to return his trophies to members of his family. It was agreed that the awards rightly belonged to him after all.

Jim Thorpe was not only a remarkable athlete, but a fighting spirit who traveled a very "Bright Path" in the eyes of sports fans everywhere.

> **Think about It**
> Why do you think these pieces of sports equipment are necessary?
> A hockey player's helmet
> A golfer's tee
> A sprinter's spikes
> A baseball player's glove
> A skier's poles

# What It Takes ★

Tips from the Champs on How to Be a Winner

**Competitive Drive**

How much do you want to win? Are you willing to keep trying when others say it can't be done? Mary Lou Retton, a powerful little gymnast from West Virginia, was only sixteen when she won her gold medal in the 1984 Olympics. She needed a score of 9.95 in the vaulting competition to tie; she needed a perfect 10 to win. The pressure was terrific. But Mary Lou said, "I welcome the added pressure. It makes me fight even more." She scored not just one, but two perfect 10s on her vaults.

"Nobody thought it could be done," said Mary Lou, "but I did it."

# The Games

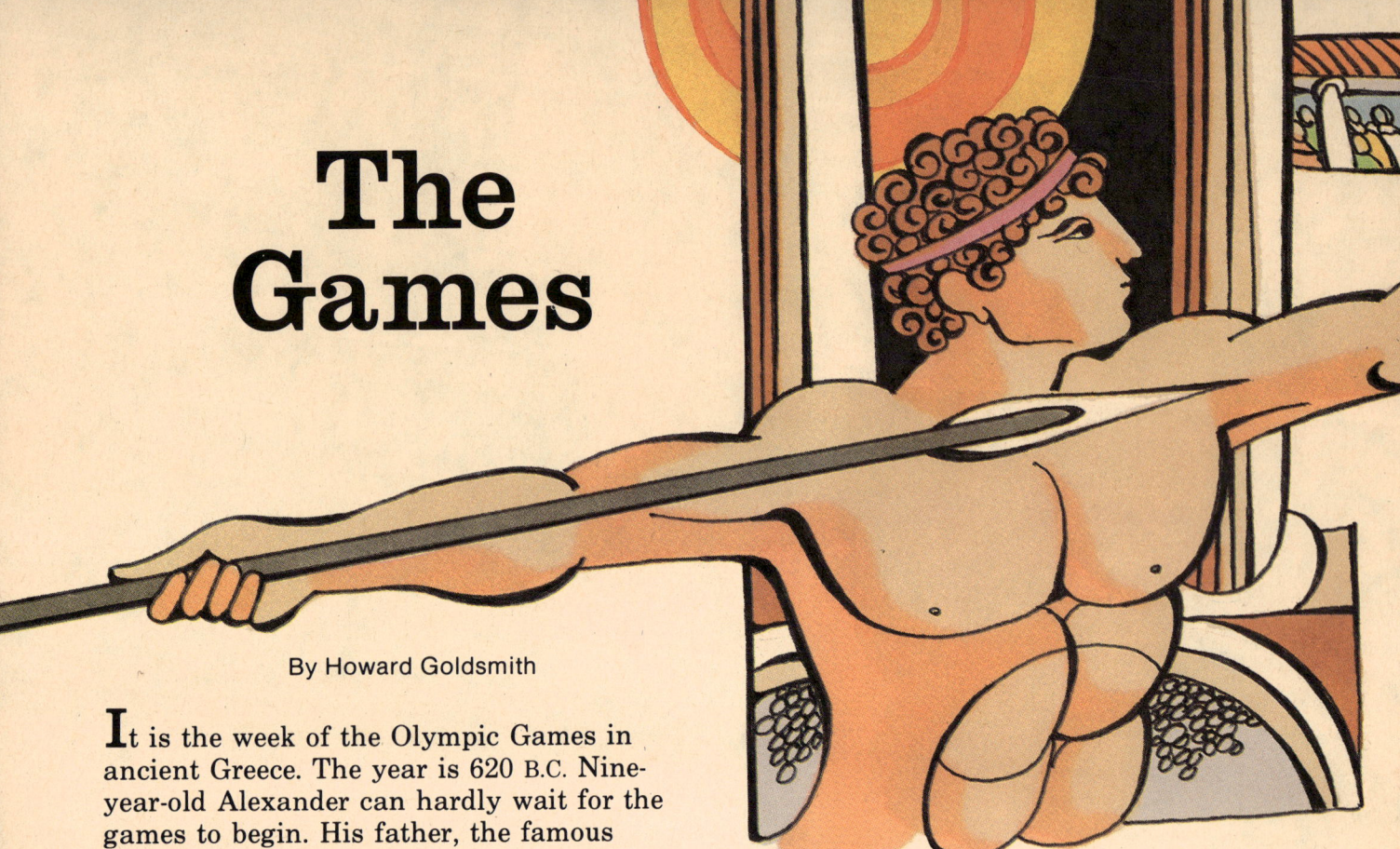

By Howard Goldsmith

It is the week of the Olympic Games in ancient Greece. The year is 620 B.C. Nine-year-old Alexander can hardly wait for the games to begin. His father, the famous athlete Leonidas, is competing in the trials.

For ten months Alexander has watched his father train for the Olympics. With pride in his eyes he has seen his father race and leap and hurl the discus from dawn to dusk. And now, at last, the games are set to begin. It is only an hour before the judges will signal the first event.

Athletes from all parts of Greece have come to Olympia to vie for honors. The winners will be crowned with laurel wreaths and celebrated throughout Greece. Poets will sing their praises in specially written poems called odes. Sculptors will carve their images in stone or cast bronze busts.

The city has been the scene of a festival for the past month. Hundreds of tents have been erected to house the contestants. Thousands of booths line the plains of Olympia, where vendors sell their wares. Outside the booths, acrobats and jugglers perform tricks to attract customers. There are even fire-eaters and sword-swallowers.

The market is teeming with people. Everyone is at a fever pitch of excitement.

Alexander is counting off the seconds now. In a very short time his father will enter the first event of the pentathlon. The pentathlon consists of five contests: the standing broad jump; throwing the discus, a round stone or metal plate weighing about twelve pounds; hurling the javelin or spear; a foot race covering the length of the stadium, about two hundred yards; and finally, a wrestling match.

The judges signal the beginning of the broad-jumping contest. From a standing start Leonidas leaps 11 feet. But Milo, Leonidas's chief rival, jumps 11 feet, 1 inch. He has beaten Leonidas. Alexander bows his head in disappointment.

### Think about It

Name some ways you might warm up before playing basketball. Before running a race. Before playing tennis. Before taking part in a sport, do you need to "warm up" your brain as well?

Leonidas winks at Alexander in the stands. "Do not be sad," his eyes seem to say. To win the pentathlon an athlete must gain three victories, and Leonidas is determined to emerge the victor.

Straining every muscle, Leonidas heaves the discus through the air. It travels 180 feet—30 feet farther than Milo's discus.

Following the discus throw, Milo hurls the javelin. It sails through the air with a whirring sound. No one has ever seen a javelin travel so far.

Alexander holds his breath as his father prepares to throw the javelin. Leonidas sets his teeth hard and rears back, clutching the javelin firmly in his powerful grasp. His arm is as taut as a spring. Uttering a loud cry, he releases the javelin. Alexander's eyes follow it as it whistles by as straight as an arrow. Everyone wonders if it can possibly reach Milo's javelin. The javelin curves slowly downward and plunges into the ground. The judges race over to it. Leonidas's throw has surpassed Milo's by 3 inches. Alexander is overjoyed.

Leonidas has now won two contests, and Milo has won one.

Alexander is confident that his father will win the next event, the foot race, since racing is Leonidas's favorite contest. But in trying to gain a fast start, Leonidas slips and sprains his ankle. He limps off the field. Without the fleet-footed Leonidas in the race, Milo goes on to win an easy victory.

Now Leonidas and Milo have each won two contests. The deciding contest will be the wrestling match.

Alexander hopes his father's sprained ankle won't prevent him from competing in the match. He watches anxiously as Leonidas hobbles about, trying to shake off the pain.

Leonidas rubs some oil on his ankle and limps onto the wrestling mat.

Leonidas and Milo shake hands. "I am sorry about your accident," says Milo. "I hope you are not in much pain."

"It is nothing," says Leonidas. "Thank you for your concern."

The two men square off at each other. For five minutes they grapple and grunt, each exerting his strength to the utmost. The muscles ripple along the curves of their bodies. The veins stand out on their necks.

Milo seems to be weakening. Sweat streams down his flushed brow. Leonidas hurls him to the ground. He leaps upon Milo and pins his shoulders to the mat.

Leonidas is the victor! He has won the pentathlon! The audience roars with excitement. Alexander jumps up and down, shouting wildly.

A laurel wreath is placed on Leonidas's head. The crowd cheers.

Leonidas motions to Alexander in the stands. Alexander races over to him.

Leonidas takes off the crown and places it on Alexander's head. The audience laughs and claps.

"We will share this crown," says Leonidas. "Someday you will win one for yourself."

Illustrated by Allan Eitzen

# "The Gazelle" of the Olympics

By Nancy A. Young

The crowds cheered as the fast, beautiful runner burst through the tape.

"Who is she?" asked someone in the stands at the 1960 Olympic Games in Rome, Italy.

"Wilma Rudolph, from the United States," came a reply.

Like a swift and graceful gazelle, Wilma ran to set new records in those Olympic Games. Her strong legs and winning form helped her win three gold medals in track—something no other American woman had ever done.

If you had seen her run that year, you would have found it hard to believe that for many years Wilma could hardly walk. When she was a small child, a terrible illness left her crippled in one leg.

Once a week Wilma's mother took her on a long bus ride from their town of Clarksville, Tennessee, to the city of Nashville, where a doctor treated her leg. Every day at home her mother rubbed Wilma's leg and helped her exercise it. On one foot Wilma had to wear a large, special shoe. Without the shoe, she could not put weight on that foot and could get around only by hopping on the other foot.

One day, after countless trips to the doctor and years of treatment on Wilma's leg, her mother came home to a surprise. There was Wilma, barefoot, shooting a basketball into the peach basket tied at the top of a pole in the yard. On the ground lay Wilma's big shoe! At last she could run with her many brothers and sisters and friends.

And how Wilma did run! She soon ran so fast that she won race after race. She would scoot here . . . and dart there . . . with such speed that her high school track and basketball coach said she was just like a mosquito. He called her "Skeeter." The name stuck. Today some still call her that.

Wilma's running ability took her to

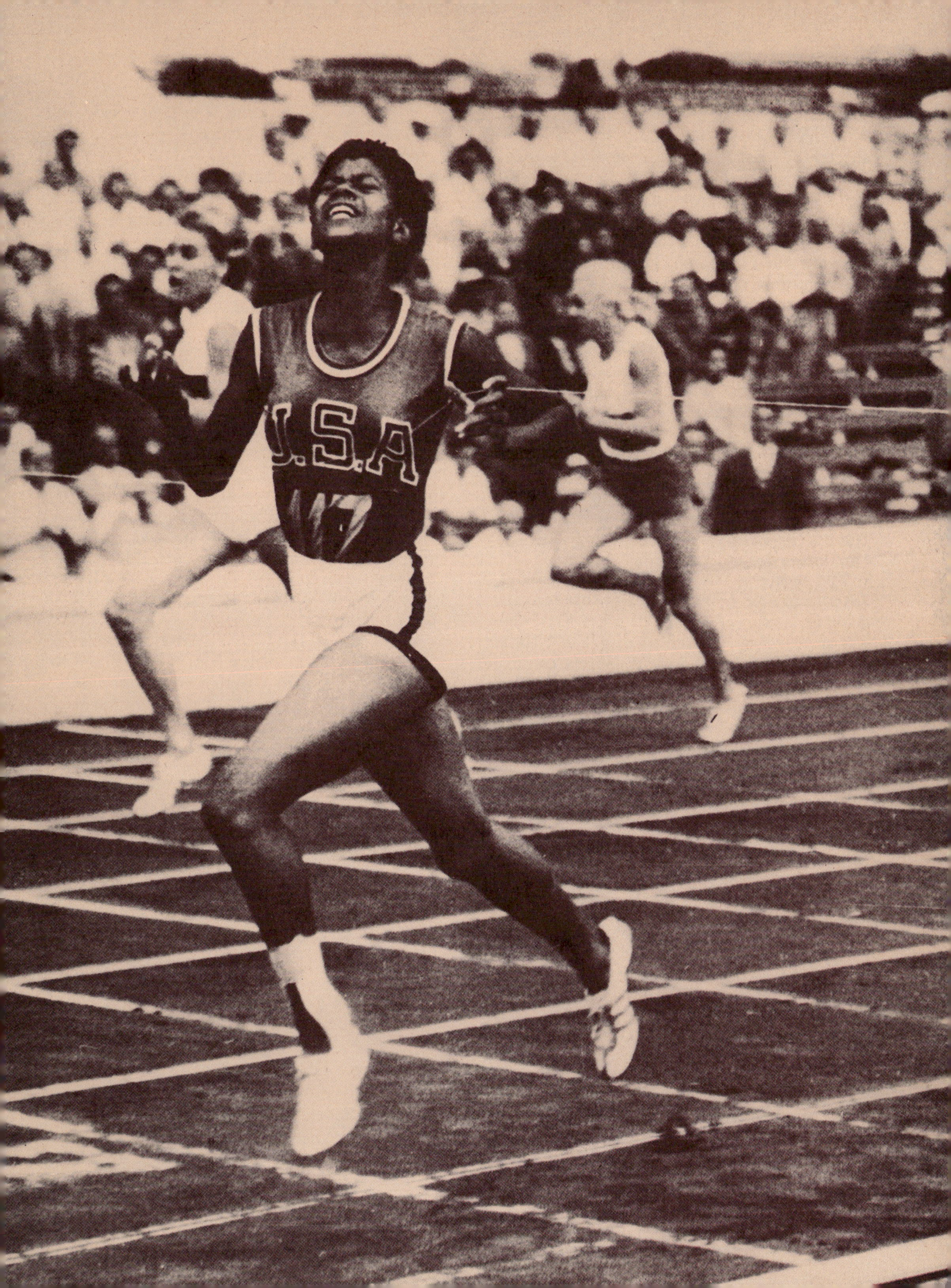
U.S.A

Tennessee State University, known for its women's track stars, the Tigerbelles. There she trained hard under Coach Ed Temple. In 1956 she made the United States Olympic team and helped the relay team win a bronze medal.

**A**t the 1960 Olympic Games in Rome, Wilma's first race was the 100-meter dash. Like a shot she was out of the starting blocks. She hit the tape three yards ahead of the runner-up and fell into the arms of a teammate. They danced with joy as the huge crowd roared and applauded. Wilma had won her first gold medal.

The graceful gazelle went on to win the 200-meter dash. A second gold medal!

There was one more race for Wilma. It was the 400-meter relay, a chance for her third gold medal. On this relay team, Wilma was the anchor runner—the runner who brings the baton to the finish line.

The runners were off. The United States team was doing fine. The first three runners built up a lead of a yard or more. But when the third runner on the team got to Wilma, the two had a bad hand-off. Wilma could not grab the baton without slowing down. By then the German runner had caught up with her. But Wilma dug in. Close to the finish she sprinted ahead and won by two yards.

When the U.S.A. team won that relay, and Wilma had won her third gold medal, everyone shouted "Wilma! Wilma!" They waved banners and threw streamers—for Wilma had won more than gold medals. She had also won the hearts of the people. They loved her smiling, winning ways, and they loved her winning runs.

**E**ver since graduating from college, which she did after the Olympics, Wilma has helped others learn to run. A few years ago she founded the Wilma Rudolph Foundation, which helps train and encourage young people in track.

"This is something I've always wanted to do," says Wilma. Through this program she gives youngsters ages five to thirteen the opportunity to run track. "We teach them a lot of different things," she says. By that, she means what it takes to be involved in a sport, and also how to make good decisions. "Just getting to know the person who lives across town," as Wilma put it, is a benefit of the program.

Wilma is grateful to her parents, coaches, and others for inspiring her. "If they had not given to me," said Wilma, "then I wouldn't be able to give to others. Track has opened hundreds of doors for me." Now Wilma is helping to open doors for others.

## Check... and Double Check!

There are at least twelve differences in the two pictures. How many can you find?

# Name Your Sport

Name the sport that belongs with each piece of sports equipment numbered below. Choose your sport from the ones listed above the equipment.

bowling skiing ice hockey
swimming golf table tennis
curling tennis badminton
croquet cricket baseball
football diving basketball

### Equipment

1. batting helmet
2. backboard
3. paddle
4. bird
5. mallet
6. pin
7. goalposts
8. broom
9. skates
10. stump
11. club
12. poles

Answers on page 48.

# Swimming Rivals

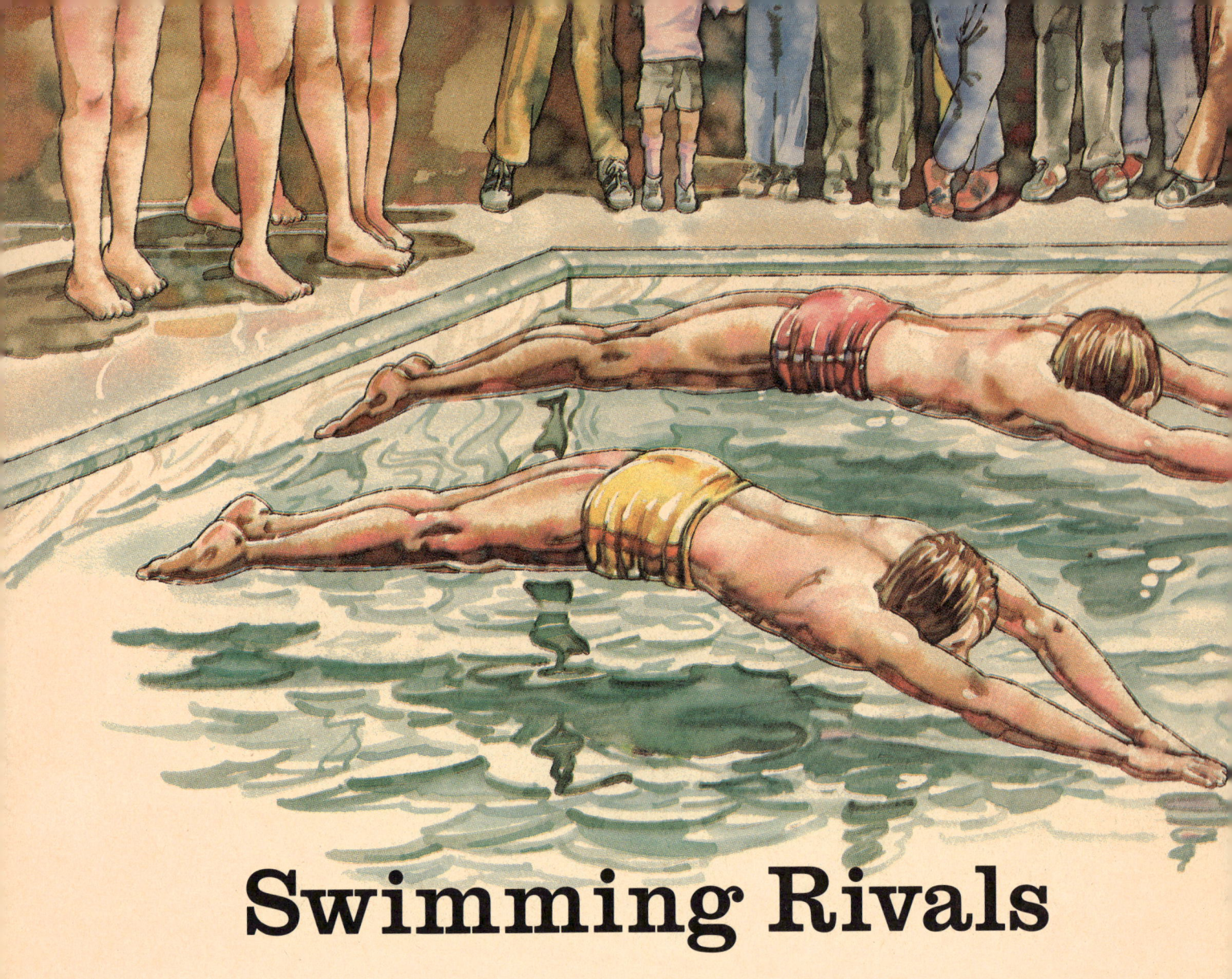

By Joseph Olgin

Billy Johnson was tense with excitement as he approached the starting line on the edge of the pool. It was the afternoon tryouts for the school's 50-yard swimming championship—two lengths of the pool. This was the race he'd been waiting for, the chance to finally beat Chet Adams.

Billy glanced over at Chet. Chet was staring straight ahead, muscles tense, waiting for the starter's gun. Billy's heart beat very fast. He was sure he was going to win this race. Even Coach Phillips said his stroke now was better than Chet's.

The gun barked. Billy plunged out into the pool with all his might. It was a perfect racing dive, shallow and very far. His arms and legs were already thrashing the water in a powerful crawl stroke as he skimmed the surface. He turned and kicked off again from the edge of the pool, using a good flip turn. A powerful push with his doubled-up legs sent him zooming ahead.

This time I win. I win, he thought. The rhythmic beat of his arms and legs seemed to sing it over and over again. "You'll win, you'll win. This time you'll win!"

Then he glanced over to the next lane to see where Chet was. His heart sank. Chet was right there beside him swimming furiously. Billy dug in hard with his arms as he forced himself through the water. The crowd roared as he pulled ahead again. There were only five yards left. He looked like a sure winner. He stole another look at Chet.

16

Chet surged forward, and they seemed to reach the pool's edge at the same moment. The race was over!

As Billy floundered about in the shallow water getting his breath back, an agony of suspense gripped him. Had he touched first? Had he finally beaten Chet?

Then an announcement crackled over the loudspeaker. "First place, Chet Adams. Second place, Bill Johnson. Third place, Tom Walters."

Billy punched the water savagely with a clenched fist. "Beaten again!"

For a long time, even after he was dressed, he just sat in the locker room and stared into space. What did he have to do to beat his rival? He had practiced until he could hardly stand, yet the result was still the same—first place, Chet Adams; second place, Billy Johnson.

Coach Phillips came over and put an arm around his shoulder. "Everybody's gone, Billy. Why don't you go home and get some rest for the finals tonight? You'll need all your strength and energy to be ready."

Billy got up slowly and groaned. "Be ready for what, Coach? Another beating?" His voice rose. "You told me I have a more powerful stroke than Chet, but . . ."

"It's true, Billy," interrupted Coach. "Your stroke is more powerful than Chet's, but Chet swims his own race without worrying about you. That's why he wins."

Billy struggled to control his voice. "What do you mean?"

Coach didn't pull any punches. "I mean if you hadn't looked over at Chet twice, you wouldn't have lost valuable yardage. There were only a few inches between you and the finish."

Billy realized that. Coach was right. He had spent more time worrying about Chet than he had his own race. He set his jaw. "Tonight I'm swimming my own race, Coach, no matter what!"

**B**illy could hardly wait for the finals. At last they were called to the starting line.

"Swimmers to your mark!" The gun barked and they were off.

Billy's racing dive was good. So was Chet's. Neck and neck, the boys swam the first 25 yards, outdistancing the rest of the swimmers. Both made their flip turns at the same moment. Not an inch seemed to separate them.

Several times Billy was tempted to look over to see where Chet was, but he fought off the impulse. This time he was swimming his own race. Dig, dig, dig, his arms and legs cut through the water. Iron bands seemed to tighten around his chest. But he fought on, forcing his leaden arms and legs to propel him through the water. Then the finish line was just ahead. Both swimmers reached out desperately to touch the end of the pool.

Billy's hand smacked the wet tiles. The race was over. His heart beat wildly as he fought for breath. He had never worked so hard. Had it been enough?

Then the announcement came over the loudspeaker. "Winner, Bill Johnson. Time 28.5. A new pool record. Second place, Chet Adams."

A little later, Coach Phillips strode into the locker room.

"I know what you have to do to beat Chet," he grinned at Billy. "Why, the answer is easy—just set a new record."

Billy put an arm around Chet's shoulders and gave him a friendly squeeze. "You're right, Coach, that's about the only way."

Illustrated by Michael O'Reilly

# On the Ball

By Geoffrey Jon Noonan

The statements on the left describe actions with a ball. Match each action with the correct game on the right.

Answers on page 48.

1. Carry the ball in your arms
2. Dribble the ball up and down
3. Throw the ball to first base
4. Roll the ball down an alley
5. Whack the ball with a club
6. Volley the ball with your friends
7. Smack the ball with your hand
8. Bounce the ball off your knee
9. Serve the ball with a racket
10. Tap the ball with a paddle

A. tennis
B. soccer
C. basketball
D. football
E. volleyball
F. bowling
G. table tennis
H. golf
I. handball
J. baseball

## Sports Safety

What safety precautions might an athlete take in hot weather?

What good are warm-up exercises?

For what sports should a player wear a mouth guard?

Can you name some sports that require players to wear gloves for safety?

Why might shoes specially designed for a sport be safer than street shoes for that sport? Give some examples.

Some athletic shoes have spikes. In what sports can these be helpful? In what sports would they be dangerous?

"I think you're in the wrong event."

# What It Takes ⭐

**Tips from the Champs on How to Be a Winner**

### Confidence

Diver Greg Louganis is a world champion. He won the gold in men's platform diving and springboard diving at the 1984 Olympics in Los Angeles, and then repeated those victories in the 1988 Games in Seoul, South Korea.

It takes confidence to climb a ten-meter platform in front of thousands of people and then make a perfect dive into the water. "When you're up there thirty-three feet above the water, and everybody's sitting out there judging *you*—that can be rough," says Greg. "You've got to have a lot of confidence in yourself." Greg believes in himself, and he proved it by being the first in fifty-six years to win Olympic titles in both platform and springboard diving.

# Rhythmic Gymnastics

By Herma Silverstein

The stage lights dim, the piano plays a happy tune, and suddenly ribbons swirl, snake, and spiral in the air. The darkened stage comes alive with soaring circles and streamers of color. When the lights brighten, the spectators gasp. Six girls—three twirling long silk ribbons and three spinning colorful hoops—are dancing to the music in synchronized ballet steps.

Elizabeth Cull of Los Angeles, California, is one of these girls. As she and two others toss their ribbons like lances, the other three fling their hoops backward over their heads. Elizabeth and her teammates ring the hoops with their arms while the other girls catch the brightly colored ribbons by sticks attached to the ends. All six girls perform the stunt without losing a single beat in their synchronized leaps, splits, and tumbling rolls.

Are they doing gymnastics? Are they doing ballet? Are they doing a juggling act? *Yes* to all the above.

These girls are performing a sport called rhythmic gymnastics, in which ballet, baton twirling, acrobatics, juggling, and synchronized gymnastic exercises are all rolled into one.

The 1984 Olympics in Los Angeles marked the first appearance of rhythmic gymnastics in Olympic competition. Yet the sport itself was first practiced by the ancient Greeks, who performed group gymnastic exercises using balls. Later Europeans practiced rhythmic gymnastics as a noncompetitive exercise. Eventually, Eastern European countries established official rules for rhythmic gymnastics, and the first world championship was held in 1963 in Budapest, Hungary.

Unlike artistic gymnastics, in which athletes perform *on* gymnasium equipment, rhythmic gymnasts perform *with* equipment—a six-meter silk ribbon, a pair of plastic clubs, a rubber ball, a hoop, and a jump rope. Except for the ribbon, one item of equipment is eliminated every season, so gymnasts actually perform only four routines in competition.

In scoring the event, judges look for originality in the dance routines and a wide variety of stunts, such as rolling, swinging, and throwing the apparatus.

A score of 10 is considered perfect, and points are deducted for such faults as stepping off the mat, dropping the equipment, getting tangled in the equipment, and—the horror of all rhythmic gymnasts— twirling the ribbon into a knot.

One of the hardest parts of rhythmic gymnastics is learning how to keep your body and the equipment moving at all times. This requires skilled eye-hand coordination. Elizabeth Cull says at first it's like patting your head with one hand while rubbing your stomach with the other.

When Elizabeth started rhythmic gymnastics, she already had some artistic gymnastic training, and three years of ballet lessons. Her coach felt she could handle being placed in a more advanced group. What a shock, however, when Elizabeth walked into the gymnasium on her first day of practice and discovered that the "advanced group" included some of the top-ranked rhythmic gymnasts in the United States!

But she soon discovered that these gymnasts had the same kind of team spirit as athletes in other sports. The girls helped Elizabeth learn the basic techniques, which not only helped her score better but also resulted in a higher overall score for her team.

Like athletes in most sports, rhythmic gymnasts learn their routines one step at a time. Elizabeth Cull spent hours just tossing the clubs and catching them, until she could catch the clubs by their long, skinny ends practically with her eyes closed. (Catching the clubs by their wide ends is a penalty.)

Although the stunts, called elements, sometimes appear easy, Elizabeth says they are actually tricky to master. "If you want to feel just how tricky," she says, "find a volleyball-sized rubber ball. Then hold one arm out to your side, and position the ball on the inside of your wrist. Let the ball roll down your arm, across your chest, and out to the wrist of your other outstretched arm. Give yourself ten points, and every time you have to touch the ball to keep it moving on course, subtract three points."

Today, as more and more young men and women take up competitive Olympic sports that require full-time training, they are often asked if they mind giving up practically all of their free time in order to practice. Elizabeth Cull expresses the viewpoint of many such athletes when she says, "I don't think about giving up my free time so much as I think about how many experiences I've been able to enjoy that I wouldn't have otherwise . . . traveling all over the world to gymnastic meets, making new friends, and feeling super when I master a new trick. Do I regret my decision to train as a competitive athlete? No way."

**The long hours of practice pay off as Elizabeth Cull demonstrates her ability before the judges.**

21

# Abebe Bikila
## Hero of the Marathon

By Jenny Beck

**W**inning a marathon is one of the hardest things an athlete can do. A marathon is 26 miles and 385 yards of nonstop running. No one can run that distance well without the courage and the determination that it takes to convince a panting, aching body to keep going.

The marathon is named in honor of Pheidippides (fi DIP ih dees), a soldier in ancient Greece who knew how to keep going. After having traveled almost 300 miles on foot to get help in a battle at Marathon, Pheidippides then had to carry news of the victory to Athens, 22 miles away. He started his run exhausted, reached Athens, gasped out the news, and fell dead.

One of the most extraordinary modern marathon runners was also a soldier. As the son of an Ethiopian shepherd, Abebe Bikila (ah BAY BAY buh KEE luh) spent many hours running in the mountains near his home. Later, when he became one of the emperor's palace guards, he kept on running regularly.

Outside of Addis Ababa, the capital city of Ethiopia, not many people had ever heard of Bikila when he entered the 1960 Summer Olympics in Rome, Italy. But two hours and fifteen minutes after the marathon began, he burst through the tape and into the circle of international superstars.

The marathon began in the Olympic stadium. After a lap around the track, the runners filed out onto the streets of Rome.

Bikila started the race in a new pair of running shoes. They soon began to hurt his feet. After only a few kilometers he pulled them off. He was used to running barefoot, and that was the way he ran the rest of the race! As he entered the stadium two hours later, Bikila was 25 seconds ahead of the next runner. The crowd rose to its feet cheering. No one they had ever heard of could run such a race barefoot, and Bikila had just run it faster than anyone else in history.

After the race Bikila turned down the cool drinks and blankets that were offered. Instead he trotted another lap around the track to cool down. Later he told reporters that Ethiopians were a poor people, not used to cars and trucks. "We run everywhere," Bikila said simply.

Four years later Abebe Bikila hoped to win a second Olympic marathon. No one had ever won two. A month before the race he had to have an operation. Experts said that there was no way that he could win.

With his smooth, steady running style that looked so easy, Bikila started out with the pack. This time the course would take him through the streets of Tokyo. When he entered the stadium at the end of the race, he was four minutes ahead of the next runner.

Long before most of the other runners had even finished the race, Bikila was on the infield grass doing sit-ups and push-ups. Many people in the stands thought that he was showing off. Those who had watched him run before knew better. Later he explained, "It's routine with me. If I don't exercise after an exhausting run, I get cramps."

He had run the race in Tokyo in two hours, twelve minutes, and eleven seconds. He had beaten his time of four years earlier, and once again no one had ever run a faster Olympic marathon.

In 1968 Abebe Bikila hoped to win a third

### The Trailblazer

Joan Benoit of the United States won the first Olympic marathon for women, claiming the gold medal in the 1984 Games in Los Angeles, California. Her time was 2 hours, 24 minutes, and 52 seconds. Prior to 1984, the longest Olympic running event for women was 1,500 meters.

Olympic marathon, this time in Mexico City. Bikila was used to running at high altitudes, for his home city of Addis Ababa, like Mexico City, is far above sea level. The thinner air (with less oxygen) would not be a problem to him as it would to most of the other runners. But at thirty-seven, he was old for an Olympic runner, was in poor health, and no one else seemed able to imagine his winning a third gold medal.

Leaving the stadium this time, Bikila quickly got to the front of the pack. He was a leader for the first third of the race, but his easy stride was gone. It was replaced by one that showed his pain. Before the halfway point, Bikila dropped out of the race, suffering from stomach cramps and a heavy cold.

After Mexico City people were sure that Bikila's days as an Olympian were over. A year later he was almost killed in a car accident. His spine was injured, and his legs were paralyzed. He would be in a wheelchair for the rest of his life. But Bikila was a true Olympian. He loved sports and decided that he would still be an athlete, even if he could never run again. In 1971 he won a medal in archery at the Paraplegic Olympics in London.

In 1972, two years before his death, Abebe Bikila went to the Olympics in Munich, West Germany. This time he went to watch as an official guest of the German government. Athletes from around the world came to greet him in the Olympic Village. They came to show respect for a true hero.

23

The Olympic Games feature the very best individual and team competition among athletes from all over the world. Volleyball player Stephen Timmons of the United States, at left, spikes the ball during a match against the Soviet Union during the 1988 Games.

Swimmer Janet Evans of the United States, below, celebrates after winning an Olympic gold medal.

Track and field is always one of the highlights of the Olympic Games. Hurdler Edwin Moses, left, and long jumper Jackie Joyner-Kersee, above, are Olympic champions.

# Be a Better Sprinter

By Thomas Horton

On your mark. Get set. Go!

In a split second you're off and sprinting down the track. Faster and faster you run toward the finish line. Suddenly a faster runner streaks by you and wins the race. Afterward, you say to yourself, "If only I could run faster."

Well, here's good news for you—eight tips to help you improve your speed. Practice for a couple of weeks, and see if they help you to run faster. These tips might even help you win that race next time.

Here's more good news. Running faster will not only help you get a better time in your race, it will also help you in other sports, like soccer, football, and baseball.

Sprinter Carl Lewis of the United States won gold medals in the 100-meter dash, 200-meter dash, and the long jump in the 1984 and 1988 Olympic Games. He also won a gold medal in the 400-meter relay at the 1984 Games.

1. *Run on your toes.* When the world's fastest sprinters run in a race, only the front part of each foot touches the ground. If they touched the ground with the whole foot, it would only slow them down. If you want to improve your speed, don't run flat-footed. Instead, carry the weight of your body on the front of each foot as the sprinters do.

2. *Lift your knees higher.* Concentrate on lifting your knees high when you run. The higher you lift your knees, the longer

and more powerful your strides will be. Lift and drive your knees forward as you run, and you will see your time improve in the sprints.

3. *Lean forward when you run.* Some sprinters stand straight up or lean back when they run. These bad habits will only slow you down. Try leaning slightly forward when you run. If you lean into the race, you'll be moving all your muscle power directly toward the finish line.

4. *Use your arms to drive you forward.* The faster you move your arms, the faster you'll be able to move your legs. Powerful arm action can help you run faster. When you run, drive your arms directly forward and backward, keeping your elbows bent at a ninety-degree angle. Do not swing your arms across your body. When you run, imagine you are pulling yourself down the track as you drive your arms forward and backward.

5. *Take faster strides.* Faster strides will produce faster times. A good way to practice taking faster strides is to run down gently sloping hills. As you run downhill, concentrate on moving your legs faster and faster. When you return to a level track, remember how it feels to move your legs faster. See if you are able to do it on a flat surface. If you can, it will help you improve your speed.

6. *Run in a straight line.* Some sprinters have a bad habit of weaving from side to side when they run. You should try to keep your body moving straight forward. A good way to see if you're moving straight ahead is to run beside a line on a track or a football field. Have a friend watch to see that your body is moving directly forward, not weaving from side to side.

7. *Relax when you run.* Don't get nervous and tense. When you run, make sure your neck, cheek, and face muscles are relaxed. If you can get your head muscles to relax, the rest of your body will usually follow. If you clench your hands tightly when you run, you'll tighten up your entire upper body, which is the last thing you want to do. Instead, run with your hands loose and relaxed, without allowing them to flop around.

8. *Become a speed machine.* When you run, make sure your arms, legs, and feet work together in a single, flowing motion. If you feel awkward or clumsy, slow down and practice making all the parts work together. Gradually increase your speed. Think of your body as a powerful machine that is smoothly propelling you down the track.

# Victory for Jeff

By Miriam Graham

The starting whistle shrilled. From between the red buoys, fourteen small rowboats splashed forward. The Junior Dinghy Race was on.

Jeff had a wild moment when his boat, *River Rat,* got caught in a piece of underwater drift. He freed it with his right oar and was off a minute behind the others. For a twelve-year-old he had a good stroke. The long hours of practice were showing.

"Pull, two, three . . . pull, two, three," chanted Jeff. The eleven-foot *River Rat*, its white paint gleaming in the sun, spurted ahead. He passed three dinghies.

The water frothed as oars flashed and dipped into the green river. Like a family of ladybugs scattering toward home, the racers in their orange life jackets rocketed upstream toward the white finish buoy one mile ahead.

Steadily Jeff gained on the leaders. Soon there were only two boats to pass. In another five minutes there was one. Only Ed Winters was ahead.

"Don't count on it, Ed," Jeff muttered. "I'm coming."

Ed Winters had edged him out the past two years, coming in first. Everyone who knew Ed had heard about it many times. This year Jeff had spared no effort to build muscle and staying power, for this would be his last race. The age limit was twelve.

Jeff pulled the *River Rat* toward the edge of the channel as he neared the inside curve of the river where the current was weakest. Here he could make better time. Today, though, a green runabout was in the way, crisscrossing as it explored the river. In it were a father, mother, and five children. Jeff worried when he saw how crowded the boat was.

Something else—no one, not even the smallest child, wore a life jacket!

Jeff had thought everyone knew that all small children should wear life jackets on the water. His father had taught him that adults should wear jackets, too. He said that regulations required a life jacket aboard for everyone in a boat.

Before Jeff could signal to the safety patrol boat running alongside the racers, the green runabout turned upstream and droned out of sight.

Jeff had lost time. He thought he heard oars splashing close behind. He dug his heels into the floorboards and pulled until his arms ached, driving toward the red victory flag waving from the tip of the white finish

Illustrated by Gary Undercuffler

buoy. The splashing of the oars behind died away.

Stroke by stroke, grunt by grunt, Jeff gained on Ed Winters. Ed began to get nervous. Too many times he peeked over his shoulder. That slowed him down.

**J**eff dug up an extra spurt of steam. He broke across Ed's wake, pulled alongside, and went by without looking at him. All he wanted to see was that red flag waving from the tip of the white finish buoy around the next bend.

He was fifteen feet ahead as he rounded that last bend. But what he saw there made him forget himself, Ed Winters, and the entire Junior Dinghy Race.

Fifty feet away the runabout, power lost, drifted as helplessly as a leaf in an eddy. There was danger ahead. The man at the wheel of the green boat had seen that he was in the path of a large wave that had been plowed up by a passing cruiser. He was doing his best to get his engine started so that he could head safely into the wave.

"Oh no," groaned Jeff. The motor would not start.

To his alarmed eyes, the wave was traveling with the speed of an express train. He looked around and saw Ed Winters passing, going upstream. He screamed at him.

"Ed, boat in danger! Stand by!"

Ed Winters did not look at him. He rowed steadily on toward the red victory flag.

It was scary how fast the wave approached. It caught the overloaded boat on the side, carrying it high into the air. The frightened passengers crowded to the other side. The boat, now off-balance, keeled over. Instantly, the whole family was in the water.

"Help!" cried the father. He caught the two youngest children in his arms and kicked to keep their heads above water.

"Help!" cried the mother, struggling to reach the other children.

"I'm coming," called Jeff. His oars flashed like propellers. "Keep kicking!" he shouted. He saw the runabout's bottom surfacing as two of the older boys started to swim for shore. "Stay with the boat," he called. "It's coming up." At his call they turned back, heading for a handhold on the overturned runabout.

Jeff quartered his dinghy into the big wave when it hit, riding it easily. Soon he was at the scene, lifting the dripping toddlers into the *River Rat* and placing them low in his boat. When the others had been helped to firm handholds on the boats, Jeff reached under his seat for his horn and blew until his lips were numb.

*Kutt kutt kut* came an answer. It was the safety patrol boat. How good the chatter of its motor sounded to Jeff! It glided in with cut engines, closely followed by several small cruisers. Willing hands went to work, lifting the exhausted family aboard.

The safety patrol officer laid an arm over Jeff's shoulders. "Good boy, Jeff. We'll take over from here. Sorry about your race."

Jeff looked at him in surprise. He had

forgotten the race. He sponged out the *River Rat* and headed for home.

Ed was back at the moorage showing his silver trophy when Jeff arrived. The miniature dinghy gleamed in the sun.

"Congratulations," said Jeff. "You have a good stroke."

"Same to you," said Ed. "I heard about the accident. They said you called, but I didn't hear you. Concentrating too hard, I guess. I thought you were still ahead."

Jeff believed him. Ed wasn't acting like his usual triumphant self. He looked at Jeff in a way that was hard to understand. Anyone who didn't know Ed might think that he looked as if he thought Jeff was the one who had come in first.

Ed wrapped his trophy in a piece of newspaper and put it in the corner of his bicycle basket. He hung one leg over the bar and stood for a moment digging in his pocket. When he found what he wanted, wadded and tightly rolled, he put it in Jeff's hand.

"Here," he said. "Here is something that belongs to you."

Jeff watched him pedal out of sight before he shook out the wad of cloth Ed had handed him. It was a red victory flag, streaked with a bit of white paint from the finish buoy.

# What's Wrong?

**How many things can you find wrong in this picture?**

30

# Tireless Trudy

By Margaret Hall

It was raining hard. High waves pounded at Trudy. Her muscles ached more with every stroke that she swam, and her skin was raw from hours in the cold seawater. Through the growing darkness her trainer called down to her from the boat alongside, urging her to stop swimming and climb up to the warmth and safety of the cabin. But she would not listen. She knew what she was going to do.

Gertrude Ederle was going to swim across the English Channel—more than twenty-one miles of rough seas. No woman had ever done it, and only five men had. She had failed once before, but on this night in 1926 she would not fail again.

Ten years before, on a sunny beach by their New Jersey summer home, her father had taught her to swim. Nine-year-old Trudy had learned fast. She loved swimming so much that she was determined to become a champion, even though it would mean years of hard work.

Her schoolwork and chores at home took up much of her time. Evenings were her only chance to swim. Usually she was so tired by then that she would have to force herself to practice. But to be a champion she would need this perseverance.

When Trudy was twelve, she started taking lessons at the Women's Swimming Association in New York, the largest association of its kind in the world. Her instructor taught her the eight-beat crawl, a new style of swimming that she would use to set some of her amateur world records.

Her ability to resist fatigue and her insistence on perfecting her skill led to her becoming one of the world's greatest swimmers. At the age of sixteen she won a three-mile race for female swimmers in New York Bay, defeating fifty-one rivals, including the American and British champions. A little later she set five world freestyle records. She was a gold medal winner on the U.S. Olympic team in 1924.

In 1925, when she was eighteen, Trudy decided to swim across the English Channel to prove that the new American crawl could be used for long-distance swimming. She felt it was worth the intense training and the effort it would involve.

The English Channel is calm enough for swimming for only a short time during the summer. Even then, there are strong crosscurrents, dangerous tides, fog, and waves. Storms can arise suddenly. Trudy did not succeed the first time she tried. Although her stamina and speed were called "unbelievable," many difficulties caused her to give up.

But the next summer, on August 6, 1926, she tried again. She started from Cape Gris-Nez in France early in the morning, with a smooth sea and a water temperature of 56° F. Luck was with her, for the Channel is seldom this warm.

On one of the tugboats that moved alongside her was Bill Burgess, who had swum the Channel on his nineteenth try. He was now Trudy's trainer. Her sister Margaret was also on board. They paced her strokes in the water and fed her beef broth from a baby bottle lowered on a string. This, along with a little chicken, was to be her only nourishment during the time she would spend in the sea.

Trudy wore a dark bathing suit, a thick rubber cap, and a pair of goggles to protect her eyes from the irritation of salt water. Her body was covered with grease to help keep her warm. She knew she was attempting something that the world believed no woman could ever do. But she had learned from her first attempt. She knew where she had made mistakes and what to avoid; she had an extra year of training and strength.

**Gertrude Ederle was still a teenager when she swam the English Channel**

The fine weather did not last. About noon a strong wind blew in, causing choppy waves. A heavy rain began, continuing all the rest of the way. The decks of the tugboats became too slippery for anyone to stand on. Though her trainer wanted to take Trudy out of the water, she never considered giving up, and her sister encouraged her to keep going.

Despite the rain, bonfires were lit on the beach at Dover, England. As night was falling, Trudy and her attendants spotted the fires. This was to be the toughest pull of all, to battle the threatening offshore tides. She used her fast American crawl stroke to sprint in. Almost everyone who has swum the Channel after Trudy has used this stroke. Her feet touched shore 14 hours and 31 minutes after she had begun—a world record!

As she waded ashore, she waved her bathing cap to the crowd of people who waited on the beach. With tears in his eyes, her father shouted, "Trudy, Trudy! You did it!"

For the next year Gertrude Ederle was one of the world's most celebrated women. Newspapers carried her name in their headlines, and magazines published accounts of her great swim. One article called her "Queen of the Waters." She had done what no woman had done before. She had swum the Channel in record time and found a place in history.

*Gertrude Ederle's hearing was seriously damaged by the crashing waves and cold water in the Channel. She became deaf, but went on to become a lecturer and to work with deaf children.*

### Making a Splash

Josh, Pam, Mike, Tom, and Jessica competed in the 100-meter butterfly race at the county swim meet. Use these clues to determine their order of finish. How many seconds apart did they finish?

—Josh finished ten seconds behind Jessica.
—Mike finished eight seconds ahead of Pam.
—Tom finished twelve seconds behind Josh.
—Jessica finished seventeen seconds ahead of Mike.

Answer on page 48.

## Some Who Made It

The English Channel is the arm of the sea that runs between England and France. It is about 350 miles long but only 21 miles wide at its narrowest part, the part that many swimmers have tried to cross. The distance is not what makes the swim so difficult. Tides, waves, weather, and cold water make crossing the Channel a challenge.

Considering the difficulties, it is surprising that so many people have tried the Channel swim.

Here are some who made it:

**Matthew Webb** was the first successful swimmer, in 1875. He made it in 21 hours and 45 minutes.

**Gertrude Ederle,** in 1926, was the first woman. Her time was 14 hours and 31 minutes.

**Antonio Abertondo** was the first to swim *both* ways nonstop, in 1961. He took 43 hours and 10 minutes to do it.

**Cynthia Nicholas** swam both ways nonstop in 1977, in the incredible time of 19 hours and 55 minutes. Then she did it *again*, in 1979, even faster: 19 hours and 12 minutes.

**Marcus Hooper** was 12 when he crossed in 1979.

**Abla Adel Khairi** was 13 when she swam the Channel in 1974.

## Who Runs Track?

Six friends each participate in a different sport after school. The sports they participate in are football, basketball, swimming, soccer, tennis, and track. Each person plays only one sport.

— Lee bought a new racket before school started.
— Bill wears earplugs while he is in the pool.
— After practice, Teresa helps sweep the gym floor.
— Rita hopes to be in the summer Olympics one day.
— There are only boys on the football team.
— Joann kicked in two goals in the match last week.

Who runs track?

Answer on page 48.

# The Fastest Bike

By Jim Redcay
Technical Editor of *Bicycling* magazine
and Jack Myers, Ph.D.

Cyclist Fred Markham, center, set a world record by riding "Gold Rush," designed by Gardner Martin, left, and Nathan Dean, right.

A bicycle speed record of 65.484 miles per hour was set May 11, 1986. That took some great cycling by Fred Markham, who had been a member of the United States Olympic team. His special, streamlined bicycle was designed and made by Gardner Martin, Nathan Dean, and Alan Osterbauer. They all shared a prize offered by the DuPont Corporation for the first human-powered vehicle to go faster than 65 mph over a 200-meter distance. No one could have done that on a standard bicycle. It took a special design.

The basic design of the standard bicycle hasn't changed much in the last hundred years. It is lighter. It has better tires, better brakes, better gears. But it still has the same form. Further improvements were not easy, and you do not see many changes even today.

Once people started to use bikes for racing, it didn't take long to discover the importance of air resistance. When you get to 20 mph, it's easy to feel that wind forces have become a big problem. Even before 1900, bicycle racers had learned to use the crouched-down position to reduce air resistance.

Inventors found that they could make improvements by streamlining. There were designs for various streamlined covers that allowed speeds up to a record of 31 mph in 1933. By this time bicycle racing had become a worldwide sport supervised by the *Union Cycliste Internationale*. Then the cyclists' union made an important decision. Streamlining and aerodynamic devices were banned from international racing. The union's idea was that racing ought to depend only on the power and endurance of the cyclist. If you think of it that way, then technical improvement of the bicycle is like cheating.

Actually, some small aerodynamic changes have been allowed in international bike racing. Cyclists now wear streamlined helmets and skintight suits. And the bike frame can be made in a teardrop shape instead of simple round tubing. Racing speeds have improved, and a record of 43.45 mph for a short distance on a standard racing bike was set by a Russian, Sergei Kopylov, in 1982.

Even though newer designs cannot be used in Olympic racing, inventors kept working to improve streamlining and make faster bikes. In order to supervise competition, they set up their own organization, the International Human Powered Vehicle Association, in 1976. Since then a new kind of contest has been going on: Who can build the fastest bike? In order to do that, you need a bike with the lowest air resistance, the smallest aerodynamic drag.

At 20 mph a cyclist must displace, or push aside, about 1,000 pounds of air every minute. The problem is how to do that with the least power. An ideal design would slice through the air in front and gently push it to one side. The hardest part is to get the displaced air to quietly come together again behind and just stop there. Any moving air left behind—like the wake left in water behind a motorboat—is wasted power. Wasted power causes drag.

Aerodynamic drag is not much of a problem at low speeds—say, under 10 mph. But drag becomes a greater and greater problem at higher speeds. Once you get to 20 mph on a standard bike, pedaling twice as hard will get your speed up to only about 26 mph.

Bike riders and inventors have thought of three kinds of ideas to cut down drag. First, you must streamline by using some kind of a light plastic form around bike and rider. Just adding a clear plastic shield in front can lower the drag about 20 percent. Using a complete plastic cover is even better.

A second idea is to reduce the amount of air you must move out of the way. You can get this effect by going to higher altitudes where

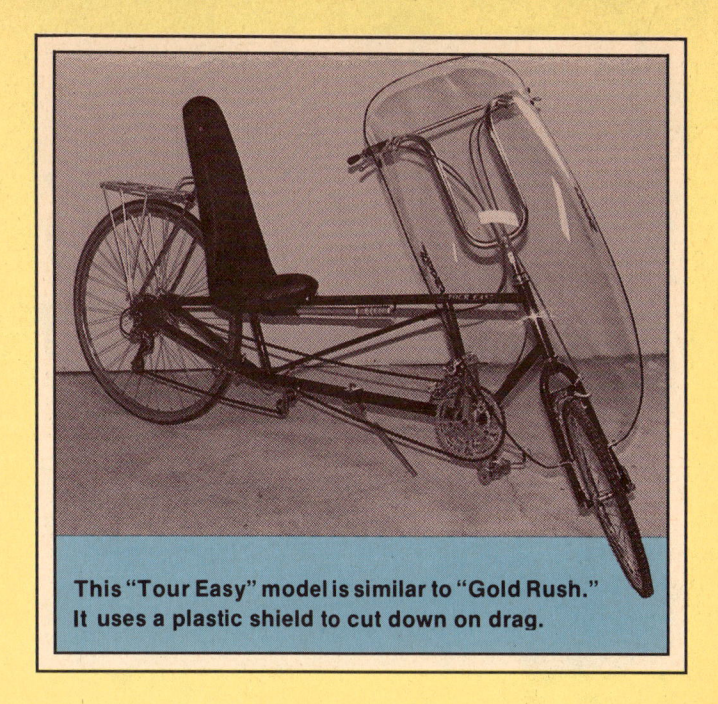

**This "Tour Easy" model is similar to "Gold Rush." It uses a plastic shield to cut down on drag.**

the air is thinner. In fact, Fred Markham's record ride was at Mono Lake, California, at an altitude of 7,800 feet. Maybe the best place of all would be on the moon where there is no air at all. Someone has figured out that on the moon, with a smooth road and a spacesuit, a cyclist on a regular bike ought to be able to go over 200 mph.

Another way to cut down on the amount of air you must move is to ride close behind another bike. Anything moving right in front of you will be dragging some air along behind it. The trick is to ride along in the airstream that is already going your way. That's like riding with a tail wind. So a team of bike riders who take turns being first can travel faster than any one of them riding alone.

There is a third idea for cutting down on drag: Redesign the whole bike so the rider is in a lying-down position close to the ground. Think about diving into water. You know that you go in easier when diving headfirst or feetfirst rather than bellyslamming. That's the idea. The very fastest bikes use the recumbent, or lying-down, position for the rider. That was the design for the Gold Rush, the special bike used by Fred Markham. He pedalled to his record while lying on his back.

Speed records are made to be broken, and we're sure there will be faster bike rides in the future. We now know the important ideas about what it takes to build faster bikes.

# Sports Laughs

**Dan:** "I sure liked my first football game. But what was all that fuss about twenty-five cents?"
**Mike:** "What do you mean?"
**Dan:** "Well, on every play, the crowd kept yelling to get the quarter back."

**Doctor:** "What do you dream about at night?"
**Patient:** "Baseball."
**Doctor:** "Don't you ever dream about anything else?"
**Patient:** "What? And miss my turn at bat?"

**Coach:** "How's Billy doing in the high jump? Any good?"
**Assistant:** "No. He can hardly clear his own throat."

The marathon runner had led the race for twenty-six miles, and was only a few hundred yards from the finish. But then he decided he was too tired to go on, so he turned around and ran back to the start.

**Waiter:** "Sir, why did you brush off your plate before you were served?"
**Diner:** "It's just a habit, I guess. I'm a baseball umpire."

**Ralph:** "Can you make a golf ball float?"
**Alice:** "Sure. Take two scoops of ice cream, add some root beer, then drop in the golf ball."

**Coach:** "Did you do your exercises this morning?"
**Sue:** "Yes. I bent over and touched my sneakers one hundred times."
**Coach:** "That sounds like a good workout."
**Sue:** "Yes. And then I took them off the chair and put them on."

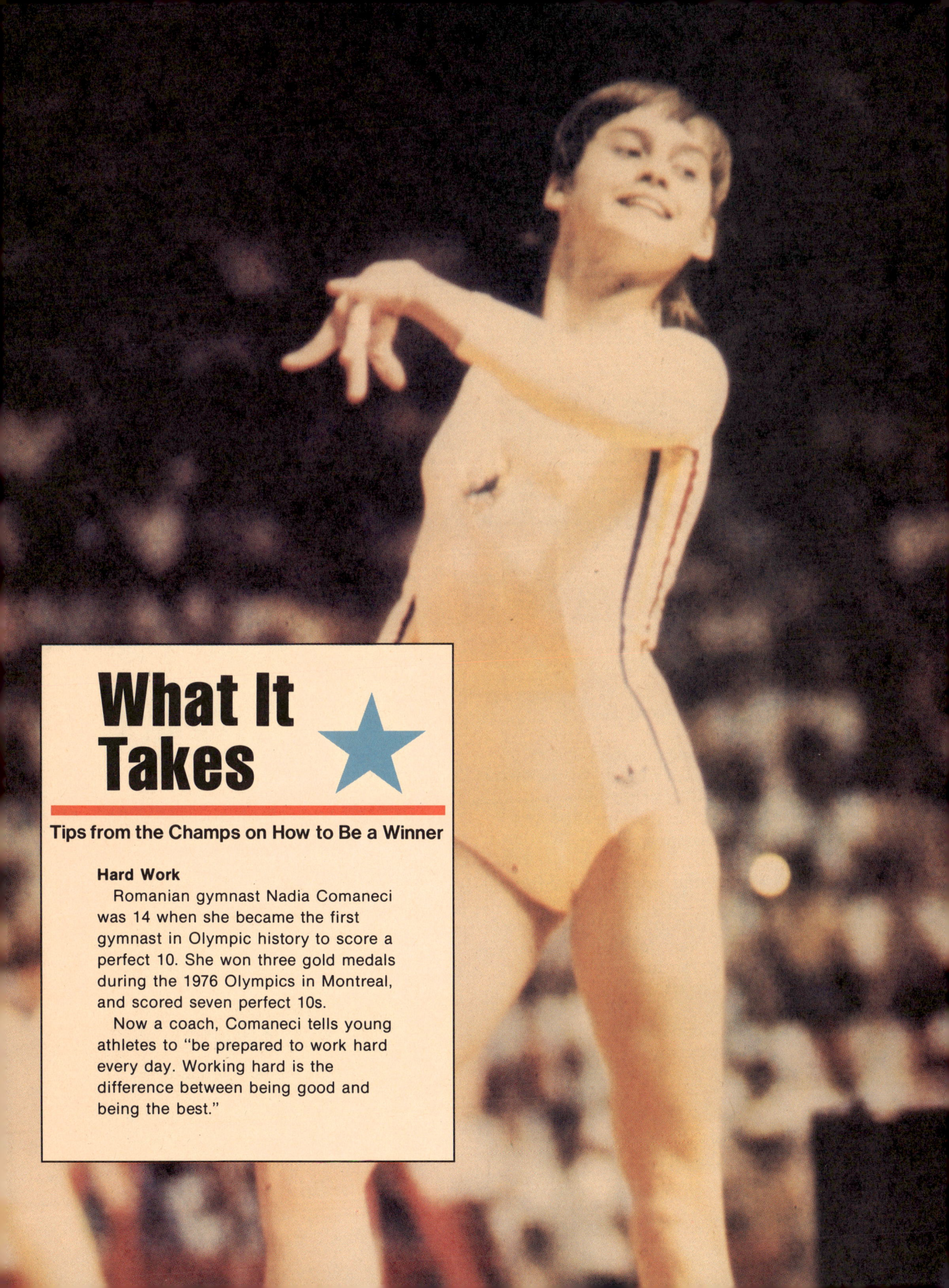

# What It Takes ★

Tips from the Champs on How to Be a Winner

**Hard Work**

Romanian gymnast Nadia Comaneci was 14 when she became the first gymnast in Olympic history to score a perfect 10. She won three gold medals during the 1976 Olympics in Montreal, and scored seven perfect 10s.

Now a coach, Comaneci tells young athletes to "be prepared to work hard every day. Working hard is the difference between being good and being the best."

# Jan's First Meet

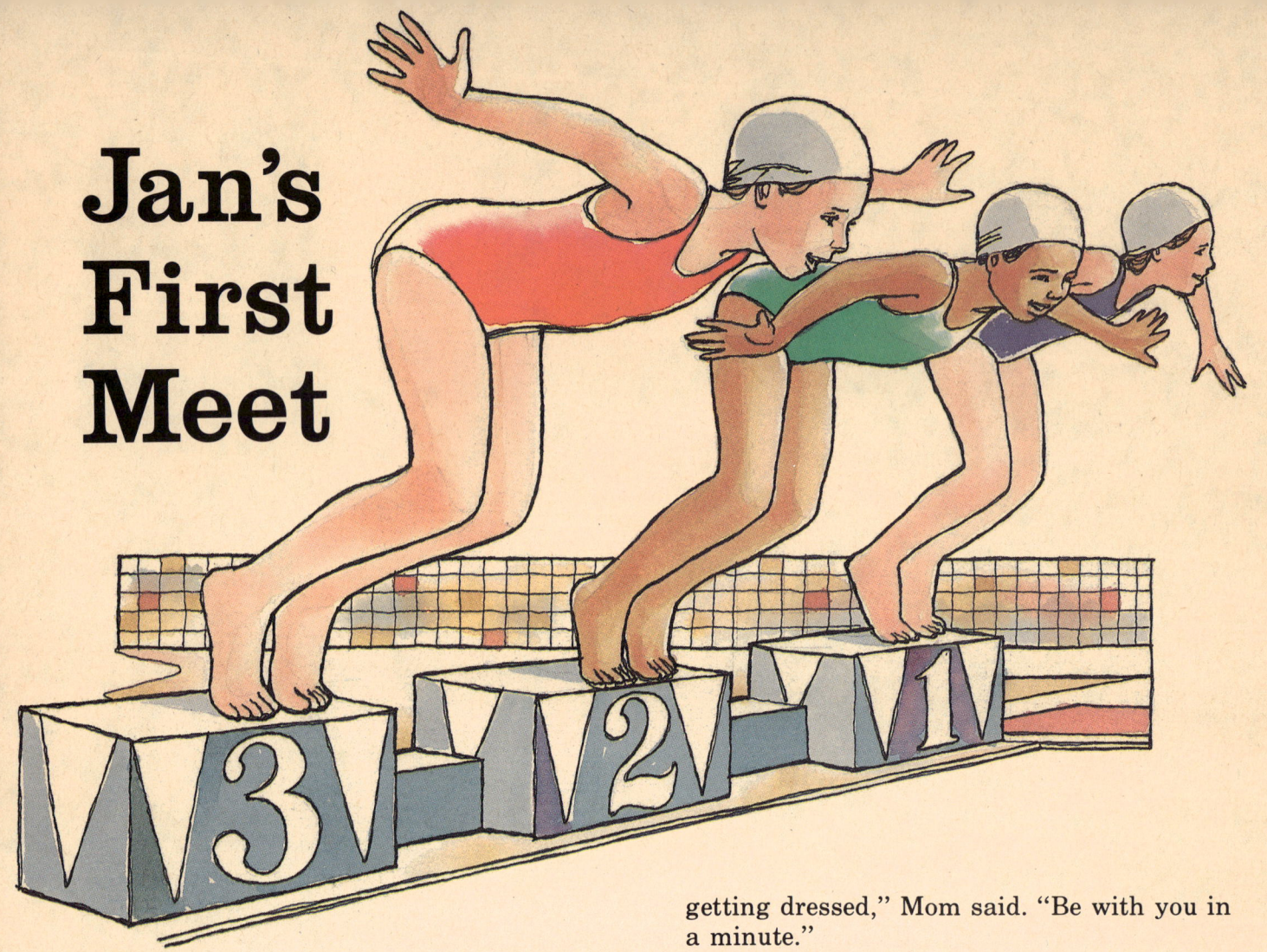

By Sidney Pozmantier

Jan shivered with excitement as she raced to her mom's car parked in front of the swim club.

"Mom, Coach said I could enter the swim meet in two weeks. I know I'll win. Wouldn't a first-place ribbon be great?"

Mrs. Reed smiled and said, "It would be super. But this will be the first meet you've entered. It takes lots of practice to win. Don't be upset if you can't do it at first."

This wasn't what Jan had expected Mom to say. "I know I can win. Well, I'm almost sure," Jan said.

The next two weeks passed too slowly for Jan. At last it was the day of the meet. *Ring* went her alarm clock, and she popped out of bed.

Then she knocked softly on Mom's bedroom door. Every other morning Mom woke *her* up. But this was different. "I'm getting dressed," Mom said. "Be with you in a minute."

Darkness was all around them as Jan and Mrs. Reed drove to the meet. "My, it's only 6:30," Mom said. She yawned sleepily.

"Coach said for us to be there at 7:00 to warm up," Jan answered. "And you know I like to be early!"

The water felt cold when Jan first jumped in. But after she took a few strokes, it felt warmer. Soon it was time to get out of the pool, and the meet began.

Jan got a schedule and said, "Look, my first event is at 8:30." She sat down next to her mom and cheered for her teammates while she waited for her event.

"This is the first call for the eight-year-old-and-under girls' freestyle," came the announcement.

"Good luck," Mom said as she gave Jan a hug.

Jan found a seat on the ready bench, but she couldn't sit still. "I'm glad I didn't eat any breakfast," she said to the girl who sat next to her. "My stomach is doing flip-flops as it is!"

"I know," said the other girl. "How long have you been on the team?"

"Only two months. This is my first swim meet," Jan answered. "I sure would like to win first place."

"That would be neat," the girl said. "But it's hard to do. I'll be happy if I come in third. I almost made it at my last meet."

"Really?" Jan said. "Coach said if I tried hard I could be a winner someday. But I think I can do it today."

"The next event is the eight-year-old-and-under girls' freestyle. First heat on the block, please."

Jan and four other girls walked quickly to their places.

"Swimmers, take your mark . . . set . . ." *Bang* and the race began.

Jan kicked hard. Her arms pulled and pulled. It was important to get a good start. She just had to win.

She kept her head in the water a long time. When she needed a breath, she turned her head out of the water. There was only one girl swimming near her.

All the rest must be ahead, she thought. I have to catch up. She kicked harder and harder.

The next time she raised her head, there was no one in sight. Jan strained every part of her body. Soon her arms began to ache, and her legs felt very heavy. "I'm not sure I can even make it to the end of the pool. And I thought I could win." The next time she raised her head, she gasped for breath. Now she was battling just to finish.

Suddenly her hand touched the side of the pool. "I made it!" Jan gasped. She looked around. There was no one else in the pool. She had come in last—not first.

"Let's give a hand for the swimmer who finished her first race," said a voice over the loudspeaker. The people yelled and clapped.

"That was a good swim," Mom said. "You didn't give up."

Jan was proud. "There will be time to win ribbons later," she said.

### Scrambled Sports

Can you unscramble these sports terms? We've given you a hint by listing the sport they come from.

dwontchou (football)
oliega (hockey or soccer)
troutkies (baseball)
uplay (basketball)
slurdeh (track and field)
yobeg (golf)
mallos (skiing)

Answers on page 48.

Illustrated by Gary Undercuffler

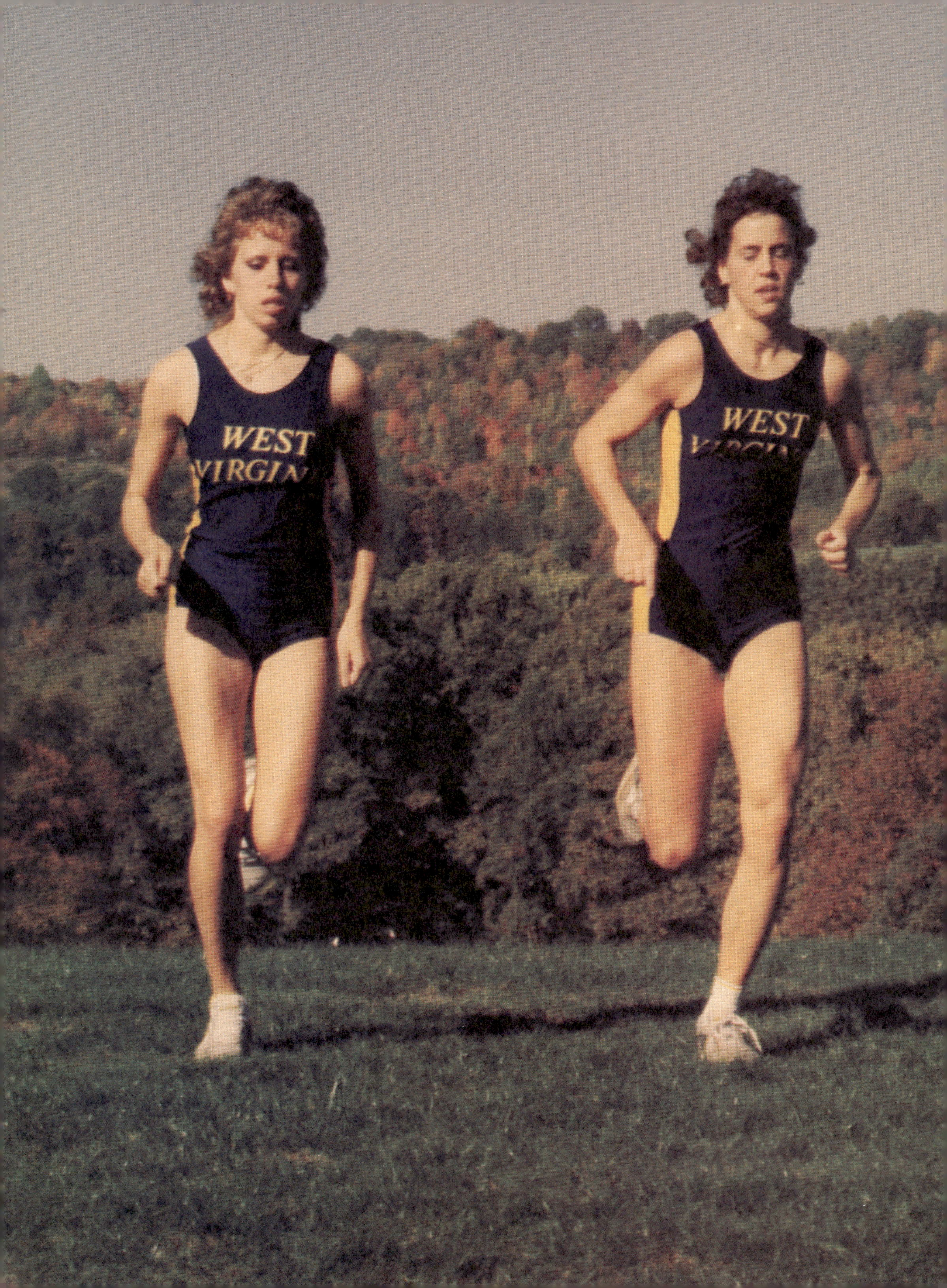
WEST
WEST

# Join the Running Generation

By Thomas Horton

Are you ready to join the running boom? If you are, then you'll be joining millions of others who already run for health, fitness, and fun.

Before you lace up your running shoes and hit the track, here are a few tips to help you get started on the right foot.

**Before you run:**

Before you start your running program, it's a good idea to get your family doctor's approval, just in case you have any problems that running might make worse. It's not necessary to go out and buy expensive equipment. Start with a good pair of running shoes, a T-shirt, and shorts.

**Your first steps:**

Find a safe place to run that is away from traffic. Parks and high school tracks are good. Avoid running on pavement if you can. Do warm-up exercises for five to ten minutes before each run, or start running very slowly to avoid straining your muscles.

Set a goal of running for fifteen minutes your first few times out. Stop and walk for a while if you get tired. Then start running again. Make sure you keep moving for fifteen minutes, even if you have to run-walk-run.

**Run the right way:**

People come in all shapes and sizes, so running styles differ. Run your natural way, but keep the following advice in mind:
- Stand straight and look ahead, not at your feet.
- Bend your arms slightly, and use them to drive yourself along in a smooth, rhythmic manner.
- Breathe with your mouth open.
- When your foot strikes the ground, hit first with your heel and then roll up onto your toes and push off.
- Keep your arms and shoulders relaxed.

**Take the "talk test":**

How do you know if you're running too fast? Take the talk test and find out. You should be able to talk normally while you run. Try it. If you're huffing and puffing, then your pace is too quick. Slow down until you can talk to your partner or sing a song as you run along.

**Keep in mind:**
- Run with a partner whenever you can. It's more fun, and safer, too.
- Watch out for traffic if you run on the street. Run on the left side, facing traffic.
- Beware of dogs.
- Wear warm clothes when it's cool, light clothes when it's hot.
- Wear some reflective clothing if you run at dusk or after dark, but try to run when it's light out.
- Drink plenty of liquids.
- See a doctor if you have any pain or soreness that doesn't go away after a few days.
- Avoid running right after eating.

### Check Your Balance

Balance is important in sports. Here's a quick way to test your balance. Stand barefoot on a hard floor, not a carpet. Lift one leg off the floor. Now close both eyes. Try to remain balanced without shuffling or moving your support foot. If you can stay still for more than five seconds, then you have good balance. More than ten seconds would be excellent.

**Stay with it:**

Run three or four times a week if you want to get the most from your workout. Once you can run for fifteen minutes comfortably, go up to twenty minutes until it's easy. Then move up to twenty-five minutes and finally to a half hour. Thirty minutes is about the maximum time for a young runner.

Many coaches feel that young people should not run very long distances. Anything over five miles is probably too far for a person younger than fourteen or fifteen.

## Warm-up Exercises

You will find it's a good idea to do what experienced runners do: Start out each run with some simple stretching exercises. Here are two you will find useful for "limbering up" the backs of the legs: hamstrings, calf muscles, and Achilles tendons. Hold the positions for a few seconds at a time, relax, and then repeat them. Do this for five to ten minutes. Do not stretch hard enough to hurt, and do not bounce.

When you are finished running, "warm down"—walk around a bit until your breathing is back to normal, and do some of these exercises, too.

**Stretch out your arms and place your palms against a wall. Lean forward at an angle, keeping your legs straight. Have your feet far enough away from the wall so that you feel the stretch in the back of your legs. You'll find the comfortable angle and distance with a little practice.**

**Put one leg up on a chair or other object in front of you so that it is horizontal. Grasp that knee with both hands, and gently lean forward. You will feel the stretch in the back of your legs, and some in your back muscles, too.**

# Cycle Sense

The Lakeville Cyclers Club held its monthly 20-kilometer bicycle race. Use the following clues to determine which of the seven cyclers won the race. Can you figure out the finishing places of the other six riders?

—The winner's sister came in third place.
—Ralph, Fred, and Mike are triplets.
—Cindy finished one place ahead of Jack.
—Sue races every month, but she has never finished ahead of Cindy or Alice.
—Mike has defeated Fred every time, but Fred always beats Cindy.
—Alice is an only child.
—Ralph finished three places behind Jack.

Answers on page 48.

Illustrated by Anni Matsick

## Four-Minute Man

On a windy day in May of 1954, Roger Bannister of England became the first person to run a mile in less than four minutes. Bannister's time was 3:59.4. The four-minute barrier was once thought to be unbreakable, but many runners have done it since Bannister led the way. John Walker of New Zealand has done it more than one hundred times!

"I'm slowly getting the hang of it."

# Babe Didrikson
## Champion Athlete

By Geoffrey Jon Noonan

Babe surprised the whole country at the Olympic tryouts in Evanston, Illinois. Over two hundred of the best American athletes came in teams to compete. The top team would win the national track and field championship.

Babe hurled the javelin to the summer sky and won first place, setting a world record. She charged over the hurdles and won first place, setting another world record. She leaped over the high bar and tied for first place with still another world record. She also placed first in the softball throw, the shot put, and the long jump.

Babe's team, the Texas Golden Cyclones, came in first with thirty points. A team from Illinois came in second with twenty-two points. The Illinois team had twenty-two athletes. The Golden Cyclones had only *one*. Babe Didrikson won the team championship all by herself!

It was called "the most amazing series of performances ever accomplished by any individual, male or female, in track and field history" by George Kirksey, who reported on the track championship. The year was 1932. Two weeks later Babe set more world records at the Olympic Games in Los Angeles, winning two gold medals and one silver.

Babe began her athletic training at a young age. Before she turned four, she was often chased by something bigger than she was—the neighbor's bull. When the bull would get loose, Babe would have to run fast and jump high to get away from it.

The neighbor was a fire fighter who kept a fire truck in his backyard. "I'd run and jump up on the fire truck where the bull couldn't get at me," said Babe.

Babe lived her first four years in Port Arthur, Texas, where she was born on June 26, 1911. Then her family moved about seventeen miles to Beaumont.

As a young girl, Babe liked to play on the gym that her father built. He wanted to help his seven lively children build good bodies. "He set up a regular gymnasium in the backyard," said Babe. "He put up bars for jumping and all that." Her father also made a weight-lifting device out of an old broomstick and two flatirons.

**B**abe loved to race against the streetcar that ran along the dirt road by her house. She also played in neighborhood baseball games. The boys liked to see her hit home runs. "Just like Babe Ruth," they said. "Let's call her Babe!" Although her first name was really Mildred, she liked this nickname, and was called Babe from then on.

Babe's father and mother had little money but a lot of love. "Some families don't show their love for each other," said Babe. "Ours always did. Momma and Poppa lived on for

**Babe's greatest performances were in golf and in track and field, but she excelled in a variety of sports.**

their kids, and they had that love from their kids all their lives."

"Momma was a good organizer," said Babe. "She'd divide up the work so that everything got done." Scrubbing the floors was one of Babe's chores. She liked to skate around on the soapsuds with the scrub brushes tied to her feet.

When she was about twelve, Babe worked at a job sewing potato sacks. "I'd keep a

45

nickel or a dime for myself out of what I made and put the rest in Momma's sugar bowl," she said.

In high school, when Babe was told that she was too small to play on the girls' basketball team, she asked the boys' coach to help her improve her skills. He took extra time to help her. Babe listened carefully and learned all the basketball moves. Sometimes she practiced with bare feet.

Two years later, she was given the chance to play on the girls' team. Babe was the high scorer from the start, and her team was undefeated. She was selected for all-city and all-state honors.

In the summer of 1928 Babe's father read the newspaper stories about the Olympic Games. He told his children about the top athletes. Babe felt inspired. She decided to train for the 1932 Olympics.

She practiced for the hurdling event by racing over the hedges in her neighborhood. One of the neighbors even trimmed his hedge to be the same height as the six others. Babe's older sister, Lillie, ran alongside while Babe jumped. As Babe flew over the hedges, she tried to beat Lillie, who was racing on the flat.

In 1930 Babe was scouted by Coach Melvin McCombs, who worked for a company that sponsored a women's basketball team. She became their top player and was named All-America for three straight years: 1930, 1931,

**Babe's hard work and determination brought her success in every sport she tried.**

and 1932. She also trained with the company's track team.

Babe set a high goal for herself. "My goal was to be the greatest athlete that ever lived," she said. "I trained and trained and trained." At the Olympic Games the confident Babe set world records while winning the eighty-meter hurdles and the javelin throw, and she tied a world record in the high jump while placing second.

Babe later married professional wrestler George Zaharias, and became a champion golfer. She won eighty-two amateur and professional golf tournaments, and dominated the sport in the 1940s and 1950s. Before she died of cancer in 1956, Babe showed she could master many other sports, including baseball, diving, swimming, bowling, and tennis.

The Associated Press sportswriters elected Babe Didrikson Zaharias as the "Woman Athlete of the Year" in 1932, 1945, 1946, 1947, 1950, and 1954. They also selected her as the greatest female athlete of the first half of the twentieth century.

# Keeping Fit

What part of the body does each activity help the most?

How does each activity help to keep a person healthy?

Which activity would you choose to help you stay fit?

Illustrated by Anni Matsick

## Sports Talk

Can you name some sports where you might hear each of the following?

"Ball four."

"Take your mark."

"First down."

"Out of bounds."

"Fore!"

"Love—15."

"Icing the puck."

"Full-court press."

"Halftime break."

"I'm afraid Snelling's a little too light for the shot put."

# Answers

### Olympic Challenge
### Page 5
1) **b.** The first modern Olympic Games were held in Athens, Greece, in 1896. Athens was the site of the original Olympic Games which began in 776 B.C.
2) **c.** The Olympic event that includes five different sports is the pentathlon—horseback riding, fencing, swimming, target shooting, and cross-country running.
3) **d.** A foil is a lightweight sword used in fencing.
4) **b.** When a weightlifter does a snatch, he lifts the bar off the ground and above his head in one motion.
5) **a.** Lacrosse is not an event in the Olympic Games.
6) **d.** Luffing and tacking are terms used in yacht racing. Luffing means changing course to sail into the wind. Tacking is turning to port or starboard, (port is the left, starboard is the right.)
7) **c.** Players rotate in volleyball. Rotating means each player on the team moves in a clockwise direction and takes a different position. This is done each time the team gets the serve.
8) **d.** The winner in the shot put hurls the shot the longest distance within a marked area.
9) **c.** The steeplechase is not a part of the decathlon, which features ten events—the 100-meter dash, long jump, shot put, high jump, 400-meter race, 110-meter hurdles, discus throw, pole vault, javelin throw, and 1500-meter race.
10) **a.** It is a foul in water polo to hold the ball underwater when you have been tackled. Water polo is played in a pool by two teams. You score by throwing the ball into your opponent's goal.

**Scoring:** Give yourself ten points for each correct answer, and then look below to see what medal you have won.

100 points: Gold medal
60-90: Silver medal
30-50: Bronze medal
0-20 points: Keep practicing.

### Page 15
### Name Your Sport
1. batting helmet—baseball
2. backboard—basketball
3. paddle—table tennis
4. bird—badminton
5. mallet—croquet
6. pin—bowling
7. goalposts—football
8. broom—curling
9. skates—ice hockey
10. stump—cricket
11. club—golf
12. poles—skiing

### Page 18
### On the Ball
1. d  2. c  3. j  4. f  5. h  6. e  7. i  8. b
9. a  10. g

### Page 32
### Making a Splash
Jessica won the race, followed by Josh, Mike, Tom, and Pam. Jessica was ten seconds ahead of Josh, who was seven seconds ahead of Mike, who was five seconds ahead of Tom, who was three second ahead of Pam.

### Page 33
### Who Runs Track?
Rita runs track

### Page 39
### Scrambled Sports
The scrambled words are touchdown, goalie, strikeout, layup, hurdles, bogey, and slalom

### Page 43
### Cycle Sense
Mike was the winner, followed by Fred, Cindy, Jack, Alice, Sue, and Ralph